Sport and My Body

Football

Charlotte Guillain

www.raintreepublishers.co.uk
Visit our website to find out
more information about
Raintree books.

To order:

☎ Phone +44 (0) 1865 888066
🖨 Fax +44 (0) 1865 314091
💻 Visit www.raintreepublishers.co.uk

Raintree is an imprint of Capstone Global Library Limited,
a company incorporated in England and Wales having its
registered office at 7 Pilgrim Street, London, EC4V 6LB
– Registered company number: 6695582

"Raintree" is a registered trademark of Pearson Education
Limited, under licence to Capstone Global Library Limited

Edited by Siân Smith, Rebecca Rissman, and
Charlotte Guillain
Designed by Joanna Hinton-Malivoire
Picture research by Ruth Blair
Production by Duncan Gilbert
Originated by Chroma Graphics (Overseas) Pte. Ltd
Printed and bound in China by South China Printing
Company Ltd

ISBN 978 1 406 21112 2
13 12 11 10 09
10 9 8 7 6 5 4 3 2 1

British Library Cataloguing in Publication Data
Guillain, Charlotte.
    Football. -- (Sport and my body)
    1. Soccer--Physiological aspects--Juvenile literature.
    2. Soccer--Social aspects--Juvenile literature.
    I. Title II. Series
    613.7'11-dc22

Acknowledgements
We would like to thank the following for permission to
reproduce photographs: Alamy p.**15** (© Christina Ferrin);
Corbis pp.**4** (Christian Liewig), **5** (Marcus Brandt/dpa),
6 (Kevin Dodge), **8** (Ned Frisk Photography), **9** (Jim
Cummins), **11** (Fancy/Veer), **17** (MM Productions), **19** (Jon
Feingersh/zefa), **20** (Wolfgang Flamisch/zefa), **23** (MM
Productions), **23** (Marcus Brandt/dpa); Getty Images pp.**10**
(Amy Guip/Photographer's Choice), **12** (Anita van Zyl/Gallo
Images), **16** (Andrew Olney/Stone), **18**, **23** (Brad Wilson);
iStockphoto pp.**22**, **22**, **22**, **14** (© Matthew Ragen), **22**, **23**
(© Oktay Ortakcioglu); Photolibrary p.**21** (Monkey Business
Images Ltd); p.**7**, **23** (© Digital Vision); Science Photo
Library pp.**13**, **23** (GUSTOIMAGES).

Cover photograph of a football being kicked reproduced
with permission of Punchstock/Brand X Pictures. Back cover
images reproduced with permission of iStockphoto:
1. whistle; 2. shin pads (© Oktay Ortakcioglu).

Every effort has been made to contact copyright holders
of material reproduced in this book. Any omissions will be
rectified in subsequent printings if notice is given to the
publishers.

Contents

What is football? 4

How do I learn to play football? 6

How do I use my legs and feet? 8

How do I use my arms and hands? . . . 10

How do I use the rest of my body? . . . 12

What happens to my body when
   I play football? 14

How does it feel to play football? . . . 16

How do I stay safe playing football? . 18

Does playing football make
   me healthy? 20

Football equipment 22

Glossary 23

Index 24

Find out more .24

Some words are shown in bold, **like this**. You can find them in the glossary on page 23.

What is football?

Football is a game we play with a ball. People play football all around the world.

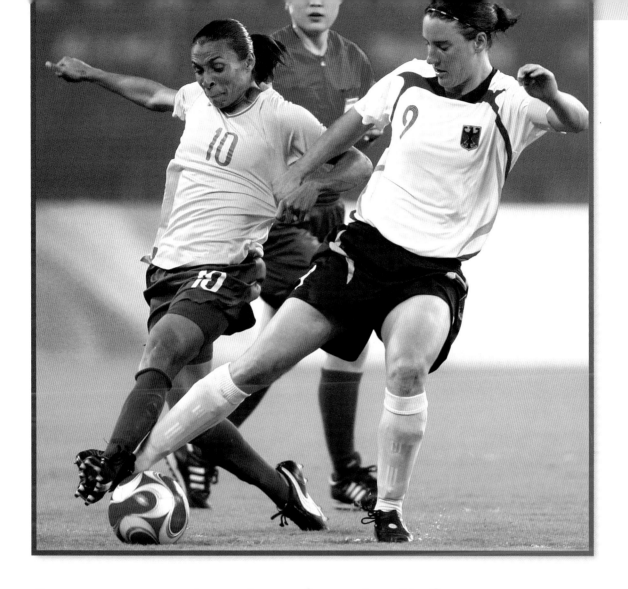

Some people play football for a team. Some people play football with their friends.

How do I learn to play football?

You can learn to play football in a park or a playground. All you need is a ball and a few friends.

You might play football at school, or in a club. A **coach** or teacher will help you.

How do I use my legs and feet?

You use your legs to run when you play football. You use your feet to **control** the ball.

You use your feet to **tackle** other players and get the ball. You kick the ball with your feet and sometimes you can score a goal.

How do I use my arms and hands?

Goalkeepers use their hands to save or catch the ball. They can stop other players scoring a goal.

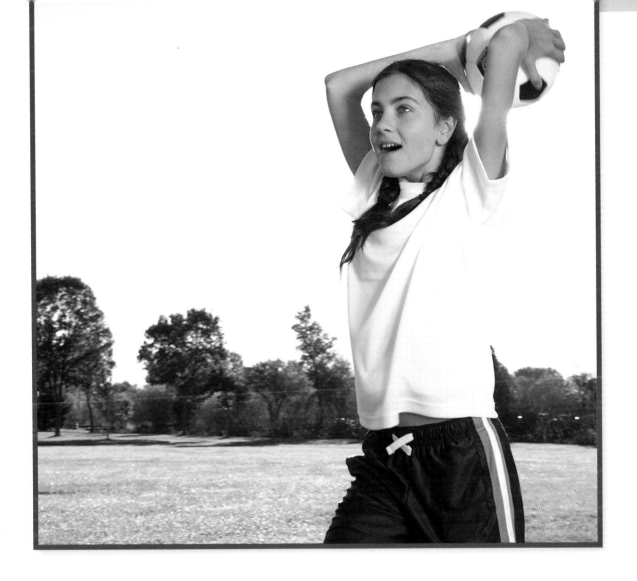

Other players can throw the ball back from the edge of the pitch. Otherwise they should not touch the ball with their hands when they play.

How do I use the rest of my body?

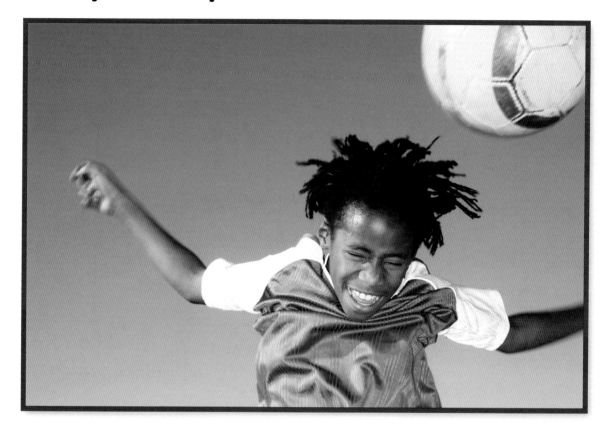

You can use your head to **control** the ball. You can also use your head to pass the ball to another player, or even shoot into the goal.

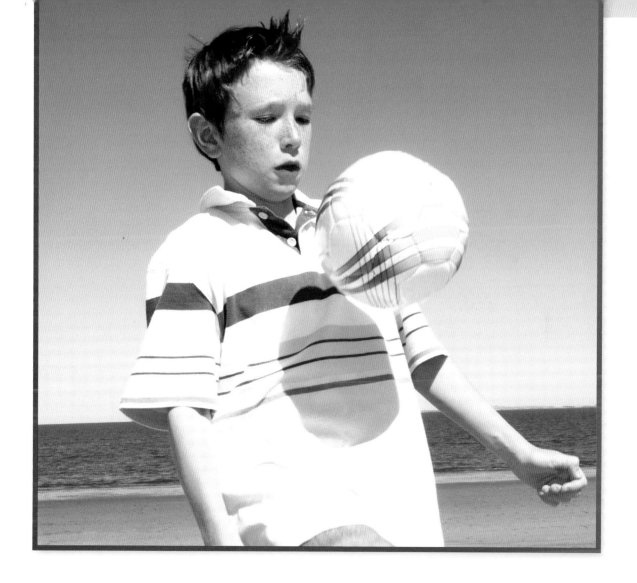

You can also use your chest to control the ball. It is easier to keep control of the ball if you watch it closely.

How does it feel to play football?

It is great to be part of a team.
It is a good feeling when you win
a game together.

You can make new friends when you play football. It is fun to play together outside in the fresh air.

How do I stay safe playing football?

You should always warm up properly before you play football. This gets your **muscles** ready to play and stops you getting hurt. You can also wear **shin pads** to stay safe.

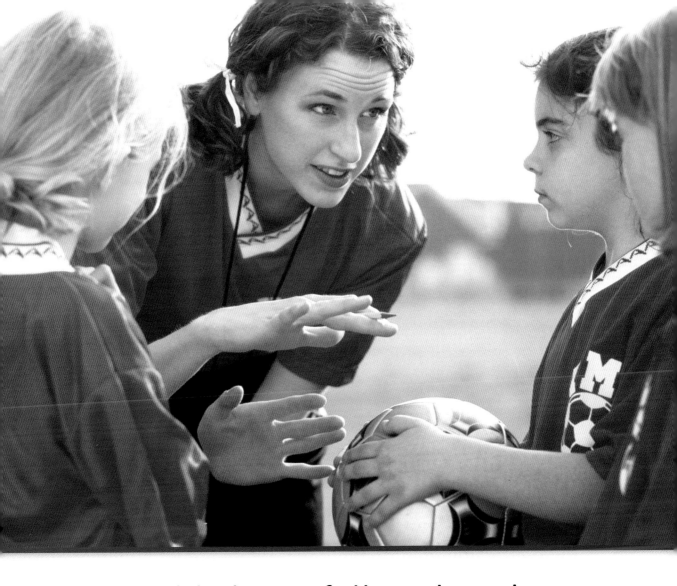

You should always follow the rules and listen to your **coach** or the **referee**. They want to keep the players safe.

Does playing football make me healthy?

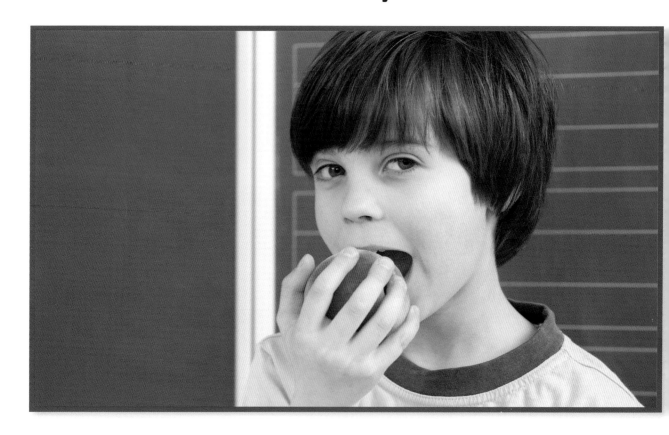

Football is good exercise and will help to keep you fit. You should also eat healthy food and drink plenty of water.

To stay healthy you need to get plenty of rest. Then you can have fun in many different ways.

Football equipment

football

football boots

shin pads

whistle

Glossary

 coach trainer. A coach helps people to learn and become better at something.

 control when you have control over something you can make it move the way you want it to

 muscle part of your body that helps you to move. Exercise can make muscles bigger and stronger.

 referee person in charge of making sure that players in a game follow the rules

 shin pad safety equipment players wear to protect their shins. Your shin is the front part of your leg below the knee.

 tackle to try and take the ball away from another player

Index

coach 7, 19, 23

control 8, 12, 13, 23

equipment 22, 23

goal 9, 10, 12

goalkeeper 10

pass 12

referee 19, 23

rules 19, 23

safety 18, 19, 23

shin pad 18, 22, 23

shoot 12

tackle 9, 23

team 5, 16

Find out more

http://www.footy4kids.co.uk
This website has lots of games for you to play to help you learn about football.

http://www.fifa.com/worldcup/index.html
Find out about the football World Cup, including photos and information about the teams.